THE WORLD OF SKATEBOARDING

TONY HAWK: SKATEBOARDING CHAMPION

Brian Wingate

the rosen publishing group's
rosen central

Dedicated to Kate and Cora

Published in 2003 by The Rosen Publishing Group, Inc.
29 East 21st Street, New York, NY 10010

Library of Congress Cataloging-in-Publication Data

Wingate, Brian.
Tony Hawk: skateboarding champion/by Brian Wingate.—1st ed.
p. cm.—(The world of skateboarding)
Includes bibliographical references (p.) and index.
Summary: A biography of Tony Hawk, the man who has invented numerous skateboarding moves and interested many, many people in this sport over the past twenty years.
ISBN 0-8239-3651-1 (lib. bdg.)
1. Hawk, Tony—Juvenile literature. 2. Skateboarders—United States—Biography—Juvenile literature. [1. Hawk, Tony. 2. Skateboarders.]
I. Title. II. Series.
GV859.813.H39 W56 2003
796.22'092—dc21

2001007615

Manufactured in the United States of America

CONTENTS

INTRODUCTION

Every sport has its heroes. These are athletes who take their game to a higher level of competitiveness. They leave their competition with their jaws hanging open in respect and disbelief. These hero-athletes blaze a trail for everyone who comes after them. They show to the world what is possible in their sport. And their achievements have an impact on their sport that will last for many years to come. Basketball has Michael Jordan. Hockey has Wayne Gretzky. And skateboarding has Tony Hawk.

Tony Hawk has been tearing up the skateboarding world for over twenty years. Along the way, and with a lot of practice, he has invented over fifty tricks. He has also turned millions of people on to the thrills of skateboarding. For Tony, it wasn't

Tony Hawk, shown here presenting an award at the *Billboard* awards with singer Pink, has taken the sport of skateboarding to new heights.

easy to become a skateboard superstar. Yet it was his dream come true.

You may have seen him on ESPN. You may have seen him land the 900 at the 1999 X Games. But how did Tony Hawk become the superstar he is today? This is his story.

1 LITTLE HAWK

Take three parts skinny, two parts wild, and add endless energy. That's Tony Hawk as a child. He looked like elbows and knees in a whirlwind. He threw toys at baby-sitters and tried to drive his parents crazy, too. Tony says in his autobiography *Hawk: Occupation: Skateboarder*, that he was a "hyper, rail-thin geek on a sugar buzz." Even when he was trying his best to drive them nuts, Tony's parents always supported him.

Tony was born on May 12, 1968. He grew up in Serra Mesa, California. He first stepped on a skateboard when he was nine years old. Back then, no one did ollies or kickflips or frontside varials. In fact, none of those tricks had even been invented yet! Most skateboarders were surfers who liked to "surf the pavement" when there were no good waves on the ocean that day.

Skateboards were more like surfboards, too. They were long and skinny and made of fiberglass. People called them banana boards.

Tony's banana board sat in the garage and collected dust for a few years. Then he started skating again with friends in the fourth grade. Around this same time, a skater in Florida named Alan "Ollie" Gelfand invented the ollie. This changed everything in skateboarding because skaters could now kick their boards into the air instead of using their hands to pick the board up. This time around, Tony was hooked. His dad, Frank Hawk, built him a ramp in the driveway.

The Amazing Ollie

Every skater today owes a special thank-you to Alan Gelfand for his creation of the amazing ollie. To do this trick, you stand on your board with your back foot on the tail. Put your front foot in the middle of the board. Slap your back foot down sharply on the tail. At the same time, move your front foot to the board's nose. Do this in a smooth move, and the front will pop up. The back will move up when your front foot slides forward. All four wheels will be in the air for an instant. No skater today could live without the ollie.

Skate Oasis

A childhood picture of Tony wearing a skateboard helmet.

Tony liked skating in his driveway. Yet there was a much bigger place that Tony wanted to skate. Hundreds of skaters tried their skills at a skatepark near his house. This park had empty swimming pools of different sizes and shapes. He could see the park from the highway and always wished that he could go inside. Finally, one day he got his wish. He spent a full day at Oasis Skatepark.

It was like a dream come true. All of Tony's energy that he used to terrorize his parents now went into skateboarding. In his autobiography, Tony says that after a full day of skating the pools at Oasis, "It was a vacuum that sucked all my energy, and for the first time in my life I actually felt . . . content. It was an alien feeling."

Tony hung out at Oasis whenever he could. His dad drove him there after school several times a week. Sometimes he had to drag Tony back home for dinner because he didn't want to leave.

Skating was hot in California in 1977. Street skating hadn't hit the scene yet, so all the best skaters were in the pools at Oasis and other parks. Skating veterans Steve Cathey, Dave Andrecht, and Eddie Elguera all skated there. Tony watched them skate and tried to learn their tricks. He skated the pools over and over.

The young Tony was so skinny that all you saw were elbows and knees when he performed his daredevil tricks.

Learning to Fly

These older skaters had one advantage over Tony that he couldn't control: their size. Most of the great skaters at the time were about six years older and seventy pounds heavier than Tony. Their extra weight gave them more speed in the flats of the pools. Tony was so skinny that he lost his momentum on flat ground. Without speed, it was much harder to pull tricks. So Tony had to adapt. What did he do? He ollied into tricks to get air.

Bones Brigade founder and champion skateboarder Stacy Peralta *(far left)* spotted Tony at a contest and offered the twelve-year-old a place on his team.

It's hard to believe now, but at that time, nobody ollied into their tricks! Most moves were started with hand grabs. Many people laughed at the sight of a scrawny kid, all elbows and knees, ollying into his tricks. Tony heard these remarks. He knew, though, that he had no choice. Ollying into his tricks allowed him to keep improving as a skater.

Tony skated whenever he could. When he couldn't skate, he thought about skating. In school, he doodled pictures of skateboards in notebooks and daydreamed of skating while staring out the window. When he finally got to the skatepark, he threw his body into skating with all his energy. He was always sporting new cuts and bruises. His shoes were held together with duct tape!

First Time Out

Tony kept practicing and entered his first competition when he was eleven. Tony was so nervous during the contest that he fell on several easy tricks. Afterward, he wasn't discouraged. He started skating more than ever. Every weekend, his dad drove him to different skateparks in the area. Before contests, he drew a picture of the course and planned out his run in his head. He planned every trick and rehearsed them in his mind. When he skated well, he was happy, but when he didn't, he was very angry with himself. Even later in his career when Tony was the star of skateboarding, his main competition was himself. He didn't care if he skated better than everyone else and won first prize. What he cared about was skating his best. If he felt that he had skated up to his full potential, then he was satisfied with the outcome of any event.

Tony kept entering contests. By the end of his first year of competition, he won first place in his age group. Then his family moved to Cardiff, California. Tony started skating a new park, Del Mar. Del Mar was only a few minutes away from their new house, so Tony's skating madness only intensified. He spent every spare moment there. He skated with the crazy abandon of an obsessed kid totally in love with a new sport. He practiced for hours—falling, getting back up, falling, getting up again—until it was time to go home. Skating was his life.

Frank Hawk, the Other Skateboard Star

Some parents freak out when their kids start skateboarding. They often sit at home and worry about injuries and falls. They may even forbid their kids from skating at all. Tony's dad, Frank, was not that kind of parent. In fact, he jumped right into the middle of the sport.

Frank Hawk never stepped on a board, but he did start two skating organizations. Each helped make the sport as popular as it is today. First, he cofounded the California Amateur Skateboard League. A few years later, he started the National Skateboard Association, which is still going strong today. Until his death from cancer in 1995, Frank was always one of Tony's biggest fans and supporters.

The Beginning of the Bones Brigade

Tony Hawk's skateboarding career really took off when he was twelve. Stacy Peralta approached Tony after a contest. Peralta was the manager of the Bones Brigade, a skating troupe, as well as the champion skateboarder in the world at the time. Peralta complimented Tony's style. A few months later, Peralta offered Tony a spot on the legendary Powell Peralta Bones Brigade. Tony would soon enter the world of professional skateboarding.

At the age of twelve, Tony accepted Peralta's invitation and joined the Bones Brigade. The Brigade was the skateboarding team for the Powell Peralta Company. Powell Peralta was one of the biggest skateboard companies in the world at the time. The Bones Brigade was named after Ray "Bones" Rodriguez, who was the first rider on the team. Tony joined skate veterans Steve Caballero, Mike McGill, and Rodney Mullen. He was the youngest skater on the team, and he soaked up skills from his older teammates. Mike and Steve were among the best skaters in the world. Tony learned as much as he could from them. Both of these older teammates were constantly on the pages of *Skateboarder* magazine. Steve was already a skateboarding god because he had invented the Caballerial (a 360-degree ollie through the air). Tricks like the Caballerial were taking everyone's skating to a new level.

Bones Brigade team member Steve Caballero, who invented the Caballerial (a 360-degree ollie through the air), was one of Tony's first skateboarding mentors.

Still Growing

Steve and Mike were five and six years older than Tony, so Tony followed them around like a little brother. They were Tony's heroes, and now he was skating with them every day! He watched and began to learn their tricks. There were some things he just couldn't do yet because of his size.

Most of the skaters on the skateboard scene still used elements of the "surfing" style. Tony couldn't build the speed to skate like everyone else. He still didn't weigh enough to keep the board moving fast enough across flat ground. He adapted by using ollies and kickflips to make new tricks like backside varials. No one had seen tricks like these before, but they soon became classic tricks of the sport.

At the time, however, some of the old-school "surfing skaters" resisted Tony's new style. What was so different about their styles? You've seen surfers carve waves in the ocean. They glide on the waves with smooth, powerful strokes, carving the water with their lower body. This same smooth style was valued in skateboarding competition at that time. Tony looked like a fish out of water when he came along and started throwing down technical tricks in every run. He brought a new kind of flow to competition. The skateboarding world was slow to catch on.

Tony joined the team as an amateur, so he didn't get any money if he won contests. This hardly mattered, though, because there was no big prize money for top skaters anyway. Most winners took home about $150. That might buy snack food for a month, but it was not enough to make a living on.

Tony worked hard to win contests. Winning contests, however, wasn't always easy. Tony struggled with his skating during his first two years on the team. Some days he tore up the course, and other times he flamed out on a new run. When he didn't skate well, he would often spend the ride home in the van staring out the window, not talking to his teammates and frustrated with his performance. He was determined to perform up to his own standards, but it took some time to adapt to the different terrain of other parks and the new challenges of life on the road.

Taking the Plunge

Tony skated with the Bones Brigade as an amateur for two years. In 1982, at the age of fourteen, Tony took the plunge. He became a professional skateboarder. He didn't know it then, but he was destined to become the most famous skateboarder in the history of the sport.

Tony's fame did not come suddenly. In fact, when Tony turned pro, hardly anyone noticed. There were no television cameras recording his moves or huge crowds shouting his name. Professional skateboarding was much smaller than it is today. Back in 1982, there were only thirty or forty professional skaters. Crowds and television cameras didn't matter to Tony anyway. He

Va Va Vert

It takes more than courage to hurtle down a twelve-foot incline on a wooden board with wheels. Some people say it takes a bit of madness—skate madness! Most skaters slowly work up to the world of vert ramps. Their steep walls can set loose a million butterflies in the stomach. Before riding a vert ramp, every skater must first learn how to fall, because it's a long way down.

lived to skate, and that was his focus. Skateboarders then didn't care about pursuing fame. They pursued fun. Tony just kept skating and trying to win contests.

Attention Getter

People still made fun of Tony because of his different skating style. His tricks were also attracting a lot of attention. During his first year as a pro, he appeared on the cover of *Thrasher* magazine doing a lien-to-tail. Tony could hardly believe his eyes when he saw himself on the cover. He had read skateboard magazines for years to see the latest tricks. Now there

Tony was only fourteen years old when he made it on the cover of *Thrasher* magazine.

he was on the front cover of one of the hottest 'zines! This attention didn't mean that everyone in the skating community quickly accepted him. Even though he was winning contests, some people still doubted Tony's ability.

More people started grumbling when Tony was declared the first champion of the National Skateboard Association (NSA) at the end of the 1983 season. Some skaters claimed that the contests were rigged because Tony's dad was the president of the NSA. Tony was surprised to win the honor because of his ups and downs throughout the year. After all the results were added up, though, he did have the highest average score. Tony

Injuries

Extreme sports like skateboarding call for extreme safety. Tony has always been careful to wear a helmet and pads whenever he skates. This attention to safety has helped Tony skate professionally for twenty years. But he has been injured, and it's hard to think of his injuries without saying "Ouch!" He has broken his elbow, knocked out his front teeth, and sprained his ankles many times. His first major injury was during his twelfth year as a pro. He had surgery on his knee after tearing cartilage. Some skaters blow out their knees or break a bone after a few months on a board. They do so because they forget to skate safely. The choice is simple: Skate safely or risk not skating at all.

knew that his dad totally supported him but that he would never bend the rules to advance his son's career. So Tony gratefully accepted the trophy and looked forward to the next year's competition. He now had to prove to everyone that he deserved the title of National Skateboard Champion.

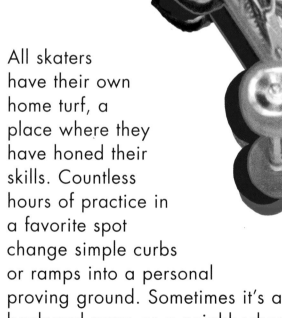

All skaters have their own home turf, a place where they have honed their skills. Countless hours of practice in a favorite spot change simple curbs or ramps into a personal proving ground. Sometimes it's a backyard ramp or a neighborhood skatepark. Other times it's a nearby public park peppered with benches and handrails. Over time, skaters know these places like the backs of their hands.

Tony's turf was Del Mar, California.

It is common for skaters to perform well on their home turf. The true test of their ability, however, is how well they skate in unfamiliar parks. Some other pros claimed that Tony could skate well only at Del Mar, since he knew the course inside and out. In fact, Tony could almost skate Del Mar in his sleep because he spent so much time there. He had skated there for years. He knew every crack, slope, and curve without needing to look. When he skated at another park, it was a different story. Sometimes he struggled to land solid runs. He returned home frustrated but determined to improve. In order to silence his critics, Tony had to prove himself on the road.

Battle in "the Badlands"

A turning point for Tony was a contest called the Upland Turkey Shoot at Upland Pipeline in California. Upland earned the name "the Badlands" because it was such a terror to skate on. Skaters competed in two connected concrete pools. One was round and the other was square, with bowls that were ten feet deep. The bottoms of the pools were rough and bumpy. It was impossible to do well without keeping momentum through the flats.

To skate at Upland, you needed much more than tricks or else you might end up eating gravel at the bottom of the pool. When his turn came to skate, Tony jumped in with all his energy. He skated hard and placed fourth. Although he didn't win first place, his performance at the Badlands sent a powerful statement to anyone who still doubted his ability. By skating well at one of the hardest parks around, he proved to himself and the world that he was more than a trick skater—he was there to stay.

Tony honed his skills at Del Mar, which he knew like the back of his hand. Others doubted him, but he proved himself at unfamiliar skateparks, too.

School Daze

Tony's skating career gained momentum. It began to carry him to new parts of the country. When he returned from the road, Tony felt stuck in high school. Tony was a bit like Clark Kent and Superman when he was in school. During the week, he was a mild-mannered kid who did well in his classes. On the weekends, he won some of the biggest skating contests in the world.

In the 1980s, skating wasn't as popular as it is today. Most people at Tony's school didn't know he was a skate star. His Powell

T-shirts and the scabs on his elbows just made Tony seem weird to the other students. He didn't make many friends at school either. All of his friends were other skaters at Del Mar. During the summers, they all hung out at Del Mar. Sometimes they even spent the night there after a full day of skating.

Hawk Takes Flight

By the time he was sixteen, many people agreed that Tony Hawk was one of the best skaters in the world. His skinny body had gained strength. He now kept his momentum on flat ground. He did tricks like airwalks and madonnas that no one else could do. He had designed his own skateboard (called a signature board) for the Powell Peralta skateboard company. After slow sales, the board was now selling well throughout America. Tony could now say he made a living as a professional skateboarder. Some of his teachers hassled him, insisting that skateboarding could not be a real career. Tony was having the time of his life, however. He got to skate all he wanted, travel the world, meet new people, and get paid for it all.

Sometimes Tony's trips took him far away from home. When Tony was fourteen, he spent the summer doing skate demonstrations. At demos, skaters get a chance to show their skills to new audiences. Many skateparks invite pro skaters to put on demonstrations on their ramps. The skaters show up at the park and skate for an hour or so. Then they sign autographs for fans and answer questions.

Tony did demos in Australia, Europe, and all over the United States and Canada. A year later, he flew to Japan to be on a television show. One summer he spent five weeks in Sweden as an instructor at a skate camp.

Fun Fact

Tony Hawk's favorite skateboard trick is a 540—two and a half rotations in the air!

Road Rules

The life of a professional skateboarder has changed a lot during Tony's career. Back when he was getting started, a skate tour was not a glamorous event. Today, thousands of people show up every year for the X Games.

Sometimes the Bones Brigade went on demo tours that lasted weeks or even months. The team drove through the night to reach the next city. Tours were different from single demos because they visited many parks instead of just one or two. If you think touring the United States for skate demos is glamorous, imagine for a moment Tony's experiences during early skate tours. It went something like this: Take a van and put eight people inside. Then put in all your skate gear covered with sweat. Drive to a new town, get out of the van, skate, spend the night in a hotel, and then move to a new town the next day. Sometimes there are ten fans waiting to see you and sometimes a few hundred.

Skate demos were hard work. Yet even with the cramped conditions and the hours on the road, Tony always had fun.

In the mid-80s, Tony's main competition came from two other top skaters, Neil Blender *(left)* and Christian Hosoi.

On Top of the World

In 1985, Tony began his senior year in high school. The popularity of skating suddenly skyrocketed, too. Crowds started pouring into the contests. Thousands of kids bought their first boards at shops across the country. Skateboarders appeared in magazine and television ads as a skateboarding wave hit the world.

Tony was riding this wave as one of skateboarding's brightest stars. Christian Hosoi, Lance Mountain, and Neil Blender were three others stars who often competed against Tony for the top prize at events.

Tony's Favorites

Tony's trips around the world have exposed him to new countries, new people, new foods, and many other new experiences. Here are a few of his favorite things.

Favorite sport to watch: Basketball
Favorite place to visit: Japan
Favorite Athlete: Lance Armstrong
Favorite Animal: Wombat
Favorite Treat: Girl Scout Thin Mint Cookies
Favorite School Subject: Math
Biggest Sports Thrill: Landing a new trick for the first time
Hobby: Producing videos

(Source: *Sports Illustrated for Kids*)

Opportunities started flooding in for Tony. He starred in a Mountain Dew commercial, and at school he suddenly became famous! Being a skater wasn't weird anymore—it was cool. Tony was no longer mild-mannered Clark Kent, he was Superman on campus.

Tony was earning thousands of dollars each month from contest earnings and royalties from skateboard sales. In fact, Tony even bought his own house! He didn't get as much schoolwork done that year. Friends always came over to skate and hang out. On the weekends, he went off to contests and returned for school on Mondays. It was challenging to balance school and his emerging career, but Tony hung in there. He earned his diploma at the end of the year.

As the crowds at competitions grew, so did the pressure to win. By 1987, at nineteen years old, Tony was the best skater in the world. Skating was at its most popular point. Up to 10,000 people came to watch contests. Tony was on top of the heap of skaters. Yet the fun was beginning to fade.

When Tony showed up to skate, everyone expected him to win. He was so good that everyone else was the underdog. Some people cheered when he missed a trick or fell on a run. Tony just wanted to skate and have fun, but participating in contests wasn't fun anymore. The pressure of winning was getting to be too much. Tony talked with his manager, Stacy Peralta, and decided to retire.

It's hard to imagine retiring at the age of nineteen, but that's exactly what Tony did. When a skater retires, though, it doesn't mean that he never picks up his board again. It just means that he will no longer skate in competitions against other skaters. Some of today's most popular skaters, like Chad Muska, haven't entered a contest in years. Nonetheless, they appear regularly in skate videos and magazines. Skaters still line up to buy their videos or catch them perform their hardest tricks at a skate demo. The bottom line should always be the same—fun. Some people thrive on the challenge of competing against other skaters. Others prefer to stay in their own backyard.

In Tony's case, his backyard was a great place to hang out. He gathered together his father and some friends and built a gigantic ramp that looked out over the California hills. This was not your ordinary backyard ramp—it cost over $30,000 to complete! Friends came over and skated all the time. He also kept himself entertained by skating in the movies *Gleaming the Cube* and *Police Academy 4*. Even though he didn't enter any contests, Tony still skated every day and worked on new tricks just like he had before.

Back in Action

Tony's retirement was short-lived. After only a few months, he felt the urge to compete again. He decided to get back into the action. He rejoined the Bones Brigade team, but this time there was something different about Tony. When he came back, he felt more relaxed. He had somehow released himself from the big pressure of winning. Now he could concentrate on the long list of tricks that he wanted to master.

Tricks of the Trade

Every new trick is a challenge. If skaters don't rise to new challenges, they can never improve their skills. Skateboarding requires patience, dedication, and skill. Even learning an ollie can take months to master. Tony has probably introduced more tricks to the sport during his career than any other skater. The 540 board

Mike McGill created the McTwist, inspiring Tony to master its flair.

varial, the 720, and the 900 are just a few examples. Each of these tricks was a challenge to learn, sometimes taking months or even years to perfect. One of the hardest tricks for Tony to learn at the beginning of his career was the 540 McTwist. Mike McGill invented the move. It's one and a half rotations of the board in the air with a flip thrown in the middle. Mike unveiled the McTwist during a competition at Del Mar. All the other vert skaters who saw it couldn't believe their eyes. A flip thrown in the middle of the spin was a revolution on the ramp!

For the next year, it seemed that every serious skater was trying to land the McTwist. Tony obsessed over it and tried the trick over and over. He focused all his energy on learning the McTwist, but it didn't come easily. Any trick can be hard on a vert ramp when you're facing a ten-foot fall. It took over two months for Tony to land his first McTwist!

Fun Fact

Tony has won twice as many competitions as any other skater.

Tony's retirement didn't last very long. By 1988, he was going as far as Australia on skate tours.

Street Style

Vert skaters weren't the only ones blazing new trails in skateboarding. Street skating ignited the possibilities of a new kind of skating in the late1980s. Skaters without access to a skatepark began doing tricks on anything nearby—benches, handrails, and even stairs. They used anything they could find. Street skaters often came up with crazy tricks that had never been done before in skateparks.

Tony tried street skating and even won some contests. He always felt more comfortable on the vert ramp, though. Street skating can be very dangerous because even one fall can lead to a serious injury. But the street-style tricks made their way into the vert world. Vert skaters started doing more technical tricks. This boosted Tony's popularity because he had always been known as a trick skater. Now technical tricks were all the rage. The tide had turned, and Tony's style was admired and respected.

Married . . . with Children

Meanwhile, Tony's personal life also gained momentum. In 1990, he got married to his long-time friend, Cindy. They met when he was in high school and stayed in touch for several years. They wrote letters back and forth and told each other what they were doing in their lives.

Tony and Cindy eventually started dating, and soon afterward, the wedding bells were ringing. In 1992, they learned of a big surprise—Cindy was pregnant! They had a healthy baby boy and named him Hudson Riley Hawk.

Street skaters brought new innovations to skateboarding, using public parks, handrails, and benches as props for tricks.

Skater Surprise

Tony was living the life of his dreams, traveling to foreign countries and skating for thousands of fans, when suddenly the bottom fell out. Skating had peaked in the late 1980s. In the early 1990s, Tony was faced with one of his greatest challenges. Skating's popularity dropped suddenly. Tony's career was threatened. Fans disappeared from contests and demos. Contest money and endorsements dried up. Tony could barely support himself as a skater. Kids began to put their money and interest into other sports and amusements.

By the 1990s, as interest declined, Tony had trouble supporting himself as a skater. Tony's love for skateboarding kept him going.

Tony had never skated for the money. He skated because had a passion for the sport. So he kept skating, and in 1991, he decided to take a chance and start his own company, Birdhouse Projects, with friend and fellow skater Per Welinder. The company's name was based on Tony's nickname, the Birdman. They made boards and recruited their own team of exciting new skaters. This happened to be at the same time that skating's popularity dropped. The company struggled to make money. Tony and Welinder weren't sure if Birdhouse was going to survive.

Tony's marriage was struggling, too. Tony was on the road a lot, and both he and Cindy felt they were growing apart. In 1994, Tony and Cindy divorced.

The 900

The 900 stands as one of the gnarliest tricks in the history of skateboarding. Tony Hawk is the only person to have ever landed it. He finally nailed the 900 at the 1999 X Games after trying on and off for thirteen years. Thirteen years! Can you imagine trying to land a trick for thirteen years? Tony fell hundreds of times trying to get it right, but the 900 stayed just out of reach.

When he landed the 900 at the X Games, the actual competition was already over. Tony wasn't skating for points or prizes, he was skating for himself. Tony could feel in his bones that the 900 was within his reach, and this time he wasn't going to let it slip away. He tried it once, twice, five times, ten times! Each time he fell. The crowd watched and cheered him on. Finally, on his twelfth time up the ramp, he flew into the air, spun around 360 degrees . . . 720 . . . and 900 . . . and landed perfectly! That's two and a half full spins through the air and back down the ramp. He raised his hands in the air and the crowd mobbed him. Skaters still try to land it today, but so far Tony is the only one to nail the 900.

X Marks the Spot

Amazingly, everything changed for Tony and professional skating in 1995. That year, ESPN aired the first Extreme Games. The sight of Tony destroying the vert ramp inspired thousands of new skating fans. After the first Extreme Games—now called the X Games—Birdhouse's sales shot up. Skateboarding was back!

The X Games helped Tony with more than just his skating career. While Tony was there, he met Erin, who was competing

The X Games revived interest in skateboarding and introduced a whole new generation to Tony Hawk's brilliance.

in the women's in-line skating competition. They hit it off and began dating after a few months. It wasn't long before wedding bells were ringing again. Tony proposed to Erin, and in September 1996, they got married. They didn't know it then, but they would soon add two sons to the Hawk family.

Once the X Games brought skating back to life, the sport raised its head like a sleeping lion. Suddenly skateboarders were in demand again. Their popularity grew all over the world. The Birdhouse team was hot, and they made a video called *The End* with each member of the team pulling unbelievable stunts. Willy Santos, Andrew Reynolds, Heath Kirchart, Jeremy Klein, Bucky Lasek, and others all light up the screen with rail slides, eye-popping stair jumps, and other crazy stunts. For his part in the video, Tony skates a gigantic ramp that sits in the middle of a bullring in Mexico. They built the ramp especially for the video, complete with a full loop at one end! You can see him skate into the loop, turn fully upside down, and zoom out the other side. It's amazing!

Though many of his competitors are a decade younger than he, Tony continues to skate, like he does here, in Middletown, Rhode Island, at a stop on a world tour.

Retired, but Still Working

In 1999, after nailing the 900 at the X Games and again at the MTV Best Trick and Highest Air event in Las Vegas, Tony decided to stop entering competitions. At thirty-one, he was ten years older than most of the pros he skated against. After such a long career in a risky sport, he was still healthy. He was also looking for new challenges. Yet it's hard to slow down after twenty years on a skateboard. So Tony didn't just skate off into the sunset. He is now branching out into other fields, such as acting and video games. He shows no signs of slowing down.

It seems as if Tony Hawk is everywhere these days. He is no longer an anonymous kid walking the halls with torn T-shirts and scabby knees. He has become an ambassador for skateboarding and a one-man powerhouse recognized throughout the world. Turn on your television and there he is, skating through a commercial during the Super Bowl. Pick up a magazine and you might find him in a milk advertisement.

A few years ago, Tony hired an agent to help him make smart business decisions. They decided to develop a television series to be shown on ESPN called *Tony Hawk's Gigantic Skatepark Tour*. Tony wanted to show his audience what life was like on a skateboard tour. The video follows Tony and a group of skaters as they tour the best parks in the United States and Canada. One of Tony's favorite stops was Kona Park in Florida.

Tony's Family

Even with his busy schedule, Tony manages to have a life outside of skateboarding. Tony is now a father of three sons—Hudson, Spencer, and Keegan. Skating will probably run in the family because his wife, Erin, used to be an ice skater and an in-line skater. Will the Hawk family become a skating dynasty? We'll have to wait and see. Hudson is already skating, and has even entered a competition at the age of seven, so watch out for another Hawk to change the face of skateboarding forever!

If it's raining outside and you still want to skate, you can always pick up one of the *Tony Hawk's ProSkater* video games and polish your skills. You can try to land the 900 in the safety of your own home.

These projects might sound like enough for one person to handle, but Tony's company, Birdhouse Projects, is not slowing down either. The Birdhouse team travels all over the world for skate demos. Birdhouse also makes a new line of boards every year.

Still Skating

Even with all these new adventures, Tony is never far from his skateboard. Although he doesn't compete anymore, he still skates whenever he can. He continues to design and ride his own boards, which are a little wider than most on the market. Skating helps him to get away from the hustle and bustle of daily life and return to the joy of learning new tricks. "Skateboarding to me means freedom," he says, "an outlet for any sort of stress and responsibilities. It's my way of expressing myself."

There is no question that Tony's gift of self-expression has changed the world of skateboarding forever. *Thrasher* magazine said in its January 1996 issue, "Never in the history of our sport has one person completely dominated it more than Hawk." Tony Hawk has raised the profile of skateboarding to an all-time high. When he started, there were just a few pro skaters making a living at the sport. Now many skaters can make a comfortable living in the sport that they love. But the joy of skating is not about the money. It is and always will be about the fun.

Tony has served as a role model for thousands of kids who want to pick up a board. With "No Skating" signs in parks everywhere, many skaters get a bad reputation as troublemakers or punks. Tony has shown the world a new face of skateboarding with his style and class on the ramps. He regularly signs up to 1,000 autographs at events for fans who drive hundreds of miles to see the Birdman fly. He wants to share the fun of the sport.

Tony always has time for the thousands of fans who show up at his events.

Skateboarding Surge

Tony must be doing a good job. Today, skateboarding is huge, and it's only getting bigger. Skateparks are springing up all over the country. In 1999 and 2000, more than 600 new skateparks were opened in the United States. Woodward Skatepark in Pennsylvania is one of the best parks ever

Tony's Quick Facts

Born: May 12, 1968
Height: 6' 3"
Weight: 170 lbs.
Marital Status: Married

created. Woodward is a 450-acre paradise with every type of ramp, bowl, and jump any skater can imagine. Every summer, thousands of people flock to Woodward from around the world to try their skills.

Slick new pros like Bob Burnquist and Andy Macdonald keep getting better and better. They are now raising the standard for the next generation. Will there be another Tony Hawk? Who will it be? Will it be you?

Flying Lessons

Everyone who skates or dreams of skating can learn from Tony's example. Skating is all about fun—and practice, practice, practice. Don't get frustrated. Learn the basics. Learn to ollie before you try to jump a flight of stairs. And if you're stoked to enter competitions, just remember that winning isn't everything. Contests don't make you a better skater than everyone else. Skating for the fun of it is the most important thing, and that is what Tony Hawk has always done so well. Tony never planned for a career in skateboarding, but he followed his dreams and passions and now the skateboarding world will never be the same. Skating was his dream, and now Tony's life is a dream come true.

GLOSSARY

airwalk A trick where the skater kicks out both legs so it looks like he or she is walking on air. Airwalks can be done while holding the nose of the board or with no hands at all.

ambassador An authorized messenger or representative.

backside A trick is backside if an obstacle is on the heel side of your board as you approach it.

backside varial A vert ramp trick where a skater reaches behind to grab the board, turns the board so the back points forward, spins the body and the board 180 degrees, and lands safely.

frontside A trick is frontside if an obstacle is on the toe side of your board as you approach it.

kickflip An ollie with a board flip thrown in the middle.

lien-to-tail In this trick, a skater comes up the ramp, grabs the nose of the board, spins, and grinds the tail of the board on the top of the ramp before heading back down the ramp.

madonna In this trick, a skater grabs the heel edge of the board and extends his or her front legs forward into the air.

ollie An essential move for most tricks. This move involves popping the board up in the air, which allows the skater to jump objects or learn many new tricks.

FOR MORE INFORMATION

Organizations

California Amateur Skateboard League (CASL)
P.O. Box 30004
San Bernardino, CA 92413
(909) 883-6176
Web site: http://www.caslusf.com

International Association of Skateboard Companies (IASC)
P.O. Box 37
Santa Barbara, CA 93116
(805) 683-5676

Web Sites

Due to the changing nature of Internet links, the Rosen Publishing Group, Inc., has developed an online list of Web sites related to the subject of this book. This site is updated regularly. Please use this link to access the list:

http://www.rosenlinks.com/wsk/thaw/

Magazines

Skateboarder Magazine
33046 Calle Aviador
San Juan Capistrano, CA 92675
Web site: http://www.skateboardermag.com

Transworld Skateboarding Magazine
Transworld Media
353 Airport Road
Oceanside, CA 92054
(760) 722-7777
Web site: http://www.skateboarding.com

FOR FURTHER READING

Burke, L. M. *Skateboarding! Surf the Pavement*. New York: The Rosen Publishing Group, Inc., 1999.

Powell, Ben. *Extreme Sports: Skateboarding*. Hauppauge, NY: Barron's Educational Series, 1999.

Ryan, Pat. *Extreme Skateboarding*. Mankato, MN: Capstone Press, 1998.

Shoemaker, Joel. *Skateboarding Streetstyle*. Mankato, MN: Capstone Press, 1995.

Werner, Doug. *Skateboarder's Start-Up: A Beginner's Guide to Skateboarding*. San Diego, CA: Start-up Sports/Tracks Publishing, 2000.

BIBLIOGRAPHY

Brooke, Michael. *The Concrete Wave:
    The History of Skateboarding.* Toronto, ON: Warwick
    Publishing, 2000.

Hawk, Tony, and Sean Mortimer. *Hawk: Occupation:
    Skateboarder.* New York: ReganBooks/HarperCollins, 2000.

Mortimer, Sean. "Board Meeting." *Sports Illustrated for Kids,* June
    2001, Volume 13, Issue 6, p. 29.

INDEX

CREDITS

About the Author

Brian Wingate lives in Nashville, Tennessee, with his wife and daughter.

Photo Credits

Cover © Tom Hauk/Allsport by Getty Images; p. 4 © VJ Lovero/Icon SMI; p. 5 © Reuters Newmedia, Inc./Corbis; p. 6 © Richard Mackson/Timepix; pp. 8, 9, 10, 13, 14, 17, 19, 24 (Christian Hosoi), 24 (Neil Blender), 28, 29, 32 © *Thrasher Magazine*; pp.12, 21© John Storey/Timepix; pp. 26, 34, 35 © Tony Donaldson/Icon SMI; pp. 31, 39 © AP/Wide World Photo; p. 36 © Jamie Squire/Allsport by Getty Images.

Design and Layout

Thomas Forget

Consulting Editor

Mark Beyer